~A BINGO BOOK~

North Dakota Bingo Book

COMPLETE BINGO GAME IN A BOOK

Written By Rebecca Stark

ISBN 978-0-87386-527-2

Educational Books 'n' Bingo

Printed in the U.S.A.

DIRECTIONS

INCLUDED:

List of Terms

Templates for Additional Terms and Clues

2 Clues per Term

30 Unique Bingo Cards

Markers

1. **Either cut apart the book or make copies of ALL the sheets. You might want to make an extra copy of the clue sheets to use for introduction and review. Keep the sheets in an envelope for easy reuse.**

2. Cut apart the call cards with terms and clues.

3. Pass out one bingo card per student. There are enough for a class of 30.

4. Pass out markers. You may cut apart the markers included in this book or use any other small items of your choice.

5. Decide whether or not you will require the entire card to be filled. Requiring the entire card to be filled provides a better review. However, if you have a short time to fill, you may prefer to have them do the just the border or some other format. Tell the class before you begin what is required.

6. There are 50 terms. Read the list before you begin. If there are any terms that have not been covered in class, you may want to read to the students the term and clues before you begin.

7. There is a blank space in the middle of each card. You can instruct the students to use it as a free space or you can write in answers to cover terms not included. Of course, in this case you would create your own clues. (Templates provided.)

8. Shuffle the cards and place them in a pile. Two or three clues are provided for each term. If you plan to play the game with the same group more than once, you might want to choose a different clue for each game. If not, you may choose to use more than one clue.

9. Be sure to keep the cards you have used for the present game in a separate pile. When a student calls, "Bingo," he or she will have to verify that the correct answers are on his or her card AND that the markers were placed in response to the proper questions. Pull out the cards that are on the student's card keeping them in the order they were used in the game. Read each clue as it was given and ask the student to identify the correct answer from his or her card.

10. If the student has the correct answers on the card AND has shown that they were marked in response to the *correct questions,* then that student is the winner and the game is over. If the student does not have the correct answers on the card OR he or she marked the answers in response to *the wrong questions,* then the game continues until there is a proper winner.

11. If you want to play again, reshuffle the cards and begin again.

Have fun!

North Dakota Bingo

TERMS INCLUDED

Agriculture (-al)

Badlands

Bismarck

Bison

Border(s)

Cattle

Climate

County (-ies)

Crops

Dakota Territory

Drift Prairie

Executive Branch

Fargo

Flag

Fort Mandan

Fur Trade

Grand Forks

Great Plains

Homestead Act

Judicial Branch

Ladybug(s)

Lake

Legislative Assembly

Lewis and Clark

Livestock

Louisiana Territory

Manufacturing

Milk

Mined

Missouri Plateau

Motto

Nokota Horse(s)

Northern Pike

Peace Garden State

Pembina

Pow-wow(s)

Prairie(s)

Railroad(s)

Red River Valley

River(s)

Theodore Roosevelt

Seal

Sioux (Siouan)

Teredo Petrified Wood

Tribes

Union

Western Meadowlark

Western Wheatgrass

White Butte

Wild Prairie Rose

Additional Terms

Choose as many additional terms as you would like and write them in the squares. Repeat each as desired.
Cut out the squares and randomly distribute them to the class.
Instruct the students to place their square on the center space of their card.

North Dakota Bingo

Clues for Additional Terms

Write three clues for each of your additional terms.

_____		_____
1.		1.
2.		2.
3.		3.
_____		_____
1.		1.
2.		2.
3.		3.
_____		_____
1.		1.
2.		2.
3.		3.

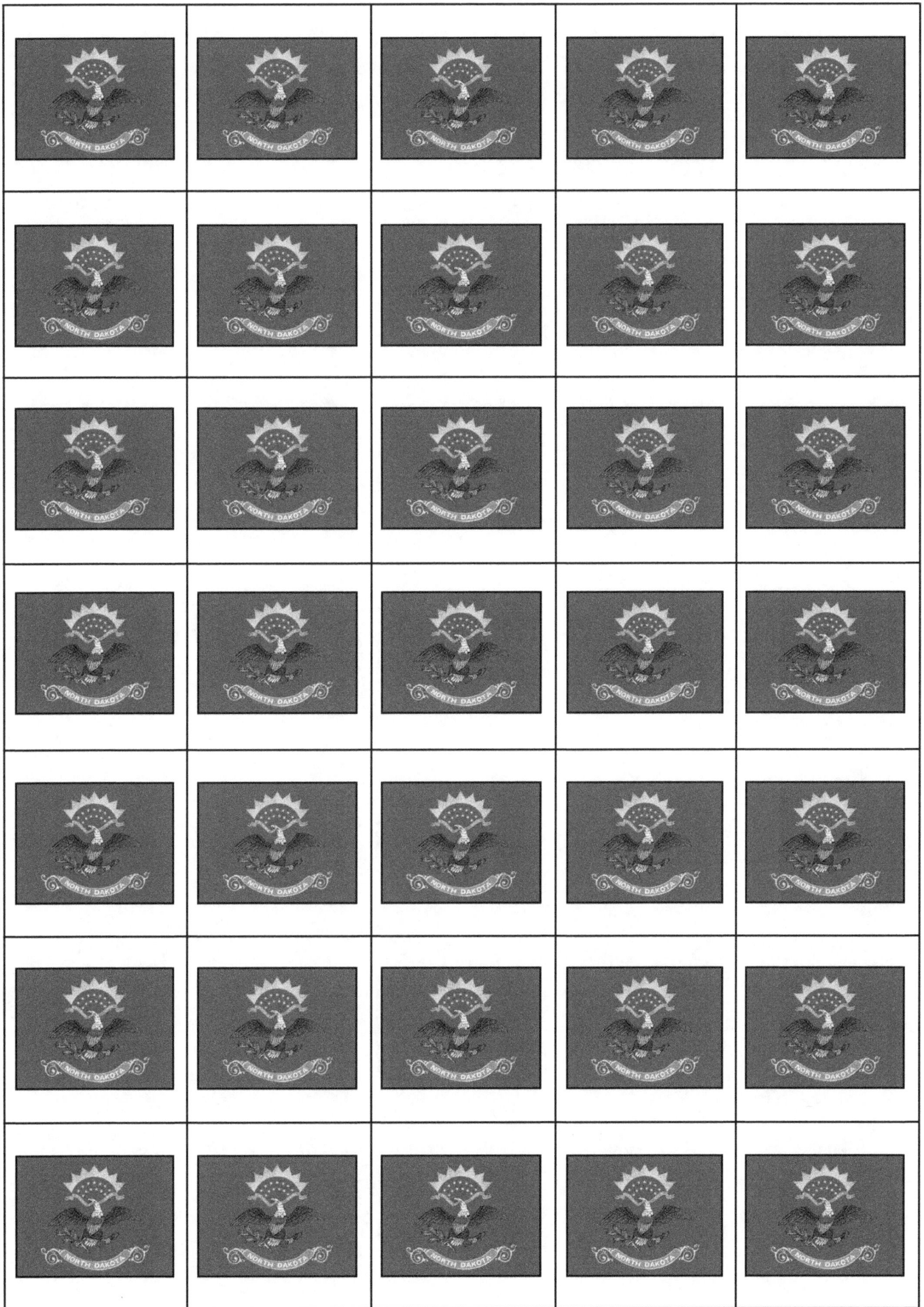

Agriculture (-al) 1. ___ production is the largest sector of North Dakota's economy. The most important ___ products are wheat, cattle and calves, soybeans, corn for grain, and sugar beets. 2. Because ___ is so important in the state, food processing is North Dakota's most important manufacturing industry.	**Badlands** 1. The ___ are in the Great Plains in areas where soft sedimentary rocks have been eroded by wind and water. The ___ of North Dakota border the Little Missouri River. 2. The ___ were carved out of the landscape by the Little Missouri River and by thousands of years of wind erosion.
Bismarck 1. ___ is the capital of North Dakota. 2. ___ is the second largest city in North Dakota after Fargo.	**Bison** 1. The American Indian tribes who lived on the plains depended on this animal for food, shelter, and clothing. 2. At one time millions of these majestic animals roamed the plains, grazing together in large herds.
Border(s) 1. South Dakota, Minnesota, and Montana ___ North Dakota. 2. Canada ___ North Dakota on the north.	**Cattle** 1. The Little Missouri River Valley was an ideal area for raising ___ because of the streams, the grasses that were good for winter grazing, and the ravines which provided shelter. 2. ___ ranching is important in North Dakota. Theodore Roosevelt had two ___ ranches in the state.
Climate 1. North Dakota has a continental ___. It is characterized by cold winters and hot summers, low humidity, and little precipitation. 2. North Dakota's ___ is affected by its location in the center of the continent. Winds move freely across the plains, causing rapid changes in temperature.	**County (-ies)** 1. There are 53 ___ in North Dakota. 2. Cass ___ is the largest. Fargo is the ___ seat.
Crops 1. North Dakota ranks high in the nation in the production of many ___, including spring wheat, durum wheat, barley, sunflowers, and many others. 2. Wheat is the most important cash ___.	**Dakota Territory** 1. ___ was created in 1861. It included much of present-day Montana and Wyoming as well as North and South Dakota. By 1868, the creation of new territories reduced it to the present boundaries of the Dakotas. 2. In 1883 the capital of ___ moved from Yankton to Bismarck.

North Dakota Bingo

Drift Prairie
1. The ___ region of North Dakota is covered by glacial deposits, or drift, which give it rich soil.
2. The ___ is the second-highest natural land region in North Dakota. This region is sometimes called the Glaciated Plains.

Executive Branch
1. The ___ comprises the governor, lt. governor, secretary of state, state auditor, attorney general, state treasurer, superintendent of public instruction, and various commissioners.
2. The governor is head of the ___. The present-day governor is [fill in].

Fargo
1. ___ is the largest city in North Dakota.
2. North Dakota State University is in ___.

Flag
1. The state ___ depicts a bald eagle holding an olive branch and a bundle of arrows. It is on a field of blue.
2. The 13 stars above the eagle on the state ___ represent the original 13 states. The ribbon in the eagle's beak has the Latin words *"E Pluribus Unum,"* meaning "Out of many, one."

Fort Mandan
1. Lewis and Clark built ___ in 1804. They spent the winter of 1804–1805 there and they returned to it on their way back east.
2. ___ provided shelter and a place of cultural interchange between the explorers and the Native Americans, for whom the fort was named.

Fur Trade
1. ___ in the area increased after Lewis and Clark described the abundance of buffalo, beaver, and river otter.
2. The French had a monopoly on the ___ in the region until 1610, when Henry Hudson discovered Hudson's Bay while sailing for England. This led to the formation of the Hudson's Bay Company.

Grand Forks
1. ___ is the third largest city in North Dakota after Fargo and Bismarck.
2. A city with the same name lies directly across from it on the other side of the Red River of the North.

Great Plains
1. The area known as the ___ covers parts of 10 states, including North Dakota; it also covers 3 Canadian provinces.
2. The southwestern part of North Dakota is covered by the ___. It is a broad expanse of flat land, much of it covered in prairie, steppe, and grassland.

Homestead Act
1. Under the terms of the ___ of 1862, a person could get 160 acres of free land by living on and improving the land for five years.
2. The ___ said that after two years, the owner could buy the land for $1.25 an acre.

Judicial Branch
1. The ___ interprets what our laws mean and makes decisions about the laws and those who break them.
2. The Supreme Court is the highest court in the ___ of the state government.

North Dakota Bingo

Ladybug(s) 1. The convergent lady beetle, commonly known as the ___, is the state insect. 2. ___ are important to the state's agriculture industry because they eat aphids, mites, and other pests.	**Lake** 1. Devils ___ is the largest natural one in North Dakota. 2. Sakakawea is the largest manmade ___ in the state. It was formed in 1960 when Garrison Dam was completed.
Legislative Assembly 1. The ___ comprises two chambers, the House of Representatives and the Senate. 2. The ___ makes the laws.	**Lewis and Clark** 1. ___ stayed longer in the region that became North Dakota than in any other place through which they traveled. 2. The ___ Expedition spent the winter of 1804–1805 with the Mandan and Hidatsa Indians. They passed through the region again in 1806 on their return from the Pacific.
Livestock 1. Beef cattle, including calves, is by far the most important ___ product. 2. Milk is the second most important___ product.	**Louisiana Territory** 1. Much of present-day North Dakota was part of the ___ , which the United States purchased from France in 1803; the rest was acquired in the Treaty of 1818. 2. ___ was renamed Missouri Territory to avoid confusion when Louisiana joined the Union in 1812.
Manufacturing (-ture) 1. Because agriculture is so important in the state, food processing is North Dakota's most important ___ industry. 2. The ___ of machinery—especially construction and farm machinery—is also an important industry.	**Milk** 1. ___ was designated the official state beverage of North Dakota in 1983. 2. The choice of ___ as the state beverage acknowledges the importance of the dairy industry to the state's economy.
Mined 1. Petroleum, coal and natural gas are important ___ products. 2. North Dakota's most valuable ___ product is petroleum. North Dakota is the fourth largest oil producing state behind Texas, Alaska, and California. North Dakota Bingo	**Missouri Plateau** 1. The ___ is the highest land region in the state. It lies west of the Drift Prairie and extends to the Montana border. 2. The eastern part of the ___ is called the Missouri *Coteau,* meaning "Little Hill." © **Barbara M. Peller**

Motto
1. The state ___ is "Liberty and Union, Now and Forever, One and Inseparable."
2. The state ___ refers to the fact that we have a free nation, which cannot be divided. This was also the ___ of the Dakota Territory.

Nokota Horse(s)
1. In 1993, the ___ was named the honorary equine, or horse, of North Dakota.
2. ___ are believed to be descendants of Chief Sitting Bull's war ponies.

Northern Pike
1. The ___ is the state fish.
2. The ___ has spiny fins and a pointed head. It can reach a length of four feet.

Peace Garden State
1. The ___ is the official nickname of North Dakota.
2. This nickname refers to the International Peace Garden on the boundary between North Dakota and the Canadian province of Manitoba.

Pembina
1. The Hudson's Bay Company established a fur-trading post on the site of present-day ___ in 1797.
2. ___ was a major fur trading post and the first European settlement in North Dakota.

Pow-wow(s)
1. ___ are an important part of the Native American culture. They are usually held in the spring to celebrate the beginning of new life.
2. The United Tribes International ___, held each September in Bismarck, is one of the largest in the United States.

Prairie(s)
1. A ___ is a large, treeless region covered with grasses and forbs, or wildflowers. Their deep underground root systems, needed because of the low amounts of precipitation, allow them to thrive.
2. The three types of ___ are tallgrass, mixed-grass, and shortgrass.

Railroad(s)
1. Fargo began to flourish after the arrival of the Northern Pacific ___; the city became known as the "Gateway to the West."
2. Before the arrival of ___ during the early 1870s, transportation in northern Dakota Territory was limited to overland travel by stage or ox cart or river travel.

Red River Valley
1. The ___ is in the eastern part of the state. The Missouri Plateau is to its west.
2. The ___ is drained by the Red River of the North. This region is extremely flat.

River(s)
1. James, Knife, Little Missouri, Missouri, Pembina, Red, Sheyenne, Souris, and Yellowstone are ___ in North Dakota.
2. The Missouri ___ is the largest ___ in the state. The Sheyenne ___ is the longest one in the state.

North Dakota Bingo

© Barbara M. Peller

Theodore Roosevelt 1. ___ National Park is located within the Little Missouri National Grassland. 2. This future President built two ranches in North Dakota: one in the Badlands and one near the boomtown of Medora.	**Seal** 1. The Great ___ depicts 3 bundles of wheat around a tree trunk, a plow, an anvil, a large hammer, a bow with three arrows, and an American Indian chasing a bison toward the setting sun. 2. Above the stars on the Great ___ is the state motto, "Liberty and Union Now and Forever, One and Inseparable."
Sioux (Siouan) 1. The Laramie Treaty of 1868 defined ___ lands as those west of the Missouri River in Dakota Territory. 2. Dakota and Lakota are ___ languages of the Great Plains. "Dakota" is a ___ word meaning "Friends" or "Allies."	**Teredo Petrified Wood** 1. ___ is the official state fossil. 2. The name ___ comes from little the clams that drilled tiny holes into the wood before it fossilized.
Tribes 1. Original inhabitants of North Dakota included the Arikara, Assiniboine, Chippewa, Hidatsa, Lakota and Dakota Sioux, and Mandan ___. 2. There are four federally recognized ___ in North Dakota: the Spirit Lake Sioux; the Arikara, Hidatsa, and Mandan Nation; the Standing Rock Sioux; and the Turtle Mountain Band of Chippewa.	**Union** 1. Both North and South Dakota were admitted to the Union on November 2, 1889. 2. No one knows which of the Dakotas was admitted first. Because North Dakota comes alphabetically before South Dakota, it is said to be the 39th state and South Dakota is said to be the 40th.
Western Meadowlark 1. The ___ is the state bird. 2. The ___ has a yellow breast with a black bib. The rest of its body is mostly brown.	**Western Wheatgrass** 1. ___ is the state grass. 2. This tough native grass once covered almost all of North Dakota. It is still found in every county of the state.
White Butte 1. ___ is the highest point in the state at 3,506 feet above sea level. 2. ___, the highest point in North Dakota, is in Slope County in the Badlands.	**Wild Prairie Rose** 1. The ___ is the state flower. 2. The ___ has five pink petals with yellow stamens in the center. It grows wild along roadsides and in pastures.

North Dakota Bingo

North Dakota Bingo

Red River Valley	Agriculture (-al)	Bismarck	Judicial Branch	Border(s)
Great Plains	Badlands	White Butte	Motto	Seal
Western Wheatgrass	Missouri Plateau		Pow-wow(s)	Wild Prairie Rose
Western Meadowlark	Theodore Roosevelt	Union	Mined	Northern Pike
Pembina	Legislative Assembly	Flag	Teredo Petrified Wood	Louisiana Territory

North Dakota Bingo: Card No. 1

North Dakota Bingo

Western Meadowlark	Western Wheatgrass	Livestock	River(s)	Milk
Northern Pike	Fort Mandan	County (-ies)	Theodore Roosevelt	Peace Garden State
Dakota Territory	Legislative Assembly		Lewis and Clark	Union
Prairie(s)	Railroad(s)	Missouri Plateau	Grand Forks	Border(s)
Seal	White Butte	Flag	Great Plains	Teredo Petrified Wood

North Dakota Bingo: Card No. 2

North Dakota Bingo

Legislative Assembly	Union	Fort Mandan	Mined	Western Wheatgrass
Northern Pike	Badlands	Crops	Agriculture (-al)	Lake
Theodore Roosevelt	White Butte		Peace Garden State	Bison
Missouri Plateau	Dakota Territory	Pembina	Prairie(s)	Livestock
Teredo Petrified Wood	Drift Prairie	Flag	Grand Forks	Milk

North Dakota Bingo: Card No. 3

North Dakota Bingo

Missouri Plateau	Peace Garden State	Bismarck	Drift Prairie	Milk
Nokota Horse(s)	Climate	Agriculture (-al)	River(s)	Western Wheatgrass
Pow-wow(s)	Prairie(s)		Louisiana Territory	Judicial Branch
Union	Badlands	White Butte	Flag	County (-ies)
Executive Branch	Seal	Cattle	Teredo Petrified Wood	Wild Prairie Rose

North Dakota Bingo: Card No. 4

North Dakota Bingo

Seal	Border(s)	Theodore Roosevelt	County (-ies)	Drift Prairie
Nokota Horse(s)	Union	Crops	Lewis and Clark	Badlands
Bismarck	Wild Prairie Rose		Motto	Ladybug(s)
Louisiana Territory	Milk	Red River Valley	Grand Forks	Fargo
Fort Mandan	Flag	Western Wheatgrass	Missouri Plateau	Pow-wow(s)

North Dakota Bingo: Card No. 5

North Dakota Bingo

Bison	Peace Garden State	Livestock	Milk	Wild Prairie Rose
Mined	Theodore Roosevelt	Fargo	Agriculture (-al)	Western Wheatgrass
River(s)	Executive Branch		Climate	Lewis and Clark
Flag	Pembina	Grand Forks	Cattle	Bismarck
Northern Pike	County (-ies)	Red River Valley	Pow-wow(s)	Fur Trade

North Dakota Bingo

Red River Valley	Peace Garden State	Ladybug(s)	Union	Fort Mandan
Northern Pike	Milk	Legislative Assembly	Badlands	Nokota Horse(s)
Wild Prairie Rose	Judicial Branch		Lewis and Clark	Climate
Missouri Plateau	Prairie(s)	Crops	Western Meadowlark	Dakota Territory
Flag	Drift Prairie	Grand Forks	Cattle	Bison

North Dakota Bingo: Card No. 7

© Barbara M. Peller

North Dakota Bingo

Pow-wow(s)	Peace Garden State	Homestead Act	Mined	Climate
Nokota Horse(s)	Bismarck	River(s)	Wild Prairie Rose	County (-ies)
Fur Trade	Drift Prairie		Milk	Border(s)
Teredo Petrified Wood	Missouri Plateau	Western Meadowlark	Executive Branch	Prairie(s)
White Butte	Flag	Cattle	Theodore Roosevelt	Northern Pike

North Dakota Bingo: Card No. 8

North Dakota Bingo

Lewis and Clark	Fort Mandan	Legislative Assembly	Fur Trade	Drift Prairie
Executive Branch	Milk	Pow-wow(s)	Theodore Roosevelt	Peace Garden State
Lake	Red River Valley		Badlands	Homestead Act
Fargo	Border(s)	Pembina	Motto	Ladybug(s)
Prairie(s)	Grand Forks	Crops	Western Meadowlark	Louisiana Territory

North Dakota Bingo

Western Meadowlark	Mined	Climate	River(s)	Fur Trade
Wild Prairie Rose	County (-ies)	Agriculture (-al)	Badlands	Milk
Drift Prairie	Peace Garden State		Judicial Branch	Dakota Territory
Pembina	Louisiana Territory	Fargo	Grand Forks	Lake
Crops	Northern Pike	Livestock	Seal	Pow-wow(s)

North Dakota Bingo

Bison	Peace Garden State	Theodore Roosevelt	Fargo	Northern Pike
Homestead Act	Lake	Motto	Lewis and Clark	Agriculture (-al)
Nokota Horse(s)	Milk		Livestock	Legislative Assembly
Crops	Western Wheatgrass	Grand Forks	Drift Prairie	Western Meadowlark
Executive Branch	Flag	Red River Valley	Cattle	Fort Mandan

North Dakota Bingo: Card No. 11

North Dakota Bingo

Fort Mandan	Border(s)	Lake	Mined	Lewis and Clark
Legislative Assembly	Northern Pike	Bismarck	Cattle	Badlands
Red River Valley	Ladybug(s)		Wild Prairie Rose	River(s)
Flag	Prairie(s)	Milk	Western Meadowlark	Nokota Horse(s)
Peace Garden State	Homestead Act	Drift Prairie	Executive Branch	County (-ies)

North Dakota Bingo

Fargo	Border(s)	Bison	Lake	Wild Prairie Rose
Bismarck	Homestead Act	Milk	Lewis and Clark	Dakota Territory
Mined	County (-ies)		Legislative Assembly	Ladybug(s)
Pow-wow(s)	Grand Forks	Climate	Drift Prairie	Western Meadowlark
Flag	Louisiana Territory	Cattle	Red River Valley	Motto

North Dakota Bingo: Card No. 13

North Dakota Bingo

Great Plains	Milk	Theodore Roosevelt	Lewis and Clark	Executive Branch
County (-ies)	Red River Valley	Lake	Badlands	Peace Garden State
Fargo	Judicial Branch		Livestock	Crops
Louisiana Territory	Grand Forks	Drift Prairie	Climate	Bison
Flag	River(s)	Dakota Territory	Northern Pike	Pow-wow(s)

North Dakota Bingo: Card No. 14

North Dakota Bingo

Motto	Lewis and Clark	Theodore Roosevelt	Fort Mandan	Mined
Bison	Livestock	Agriculture (-al)	Bismarck	Executive Branch
Wild Prairie Rose	Red River Valley		Western Wheatgrass	Peace Garden State
Flag	Lake	Homestead Act	Grand Forks	Fargo
Northern Pike	Prairie(s)	Cattle	Fur Trade	Legislative Assembly

North Dakota Bingo

Climate	Lake	Homestead Act	Fur Trade	Railroad(s)
River(s)	Dakota Territory	Ladybug(s)	Nokota Horse(s)	Judicial Branch
Fargo	Border(s)		Wild Prairie Rose	Legislative Assembly
Missouri Plateau	County (-ies)	Flag	Motto	Western Meadowlark
Executive Branch	Tribes	Cattle	Prairie(s)	Peace Garden State

North Dakota Bingo

Crops	Sioux (Siouan)	Manufacturing (-ture	Lake	Great Plains
Motto	Executive Branch	Grand Forks	Judicial Branch	Ladybug(s)
Lewis and Clark	Pow-wow(s)		Tribes	Homestead Act
Louisiana Territory	Northern Pike	Western Meadowlark	Theodore Roosevelt	Dakota Territory
Pembina	Fargo	Fort Mandan	Mined	Border(s)

North Dakota Bingo

Fur Trade	Drift Prairie	County (-ies)	Fargo	River(s)
Peace Garden State	Crops	Pembina	Wild Prairie Rose	Executive Branch
Lewis and Clark	Dakota Territory		Manufacturing (-ture)	Bismarck
Border(s)	Agriculture (-al)	Grand Forks	Western Meadowlark	Livestock
Tribes	Lake	Theodore Roosevelt	Sioux (Siouan)	Bison

North Dakota Bingo: Card No. 18

North Dakota Bingo

Wild Prairie Rose	Bison	Lake	Homestead Act	Western Meadowlark
Motto	Mined	Peace Garden State	Fort Mandan	Judicial Branch
Sioux (Siouan)	Drift Prairie		Badlands	Western Wheatgrass
Livestock	Tribes	Pembina	Prairie(s)	Manufacturing (-ture)
Bismarck	Railroad(s)	Northern Pike	Pow-wow(s)	Cattle

North Dakota Bingo: Card No. 19

North Dakota Bingo

Great Plains	Sioux (Siouan)	Mined	Lake	Cattle
County (-ies)	Legislative Assembly	Nokota Horse(s)	Pembina	River(s)
Border(s)	Ladybug(s)		Missouri Plateau	Agriculture (-al)
Seal	White Butte	Teredo Petrified Wood	Prairie(s)	Tribes
Union	Pow-wow(s)	Railroad(s)	Western Meadowlark	Manufacturing (-ture)

North Dakota Bingo

Motto	Bison	Nokota Horse(s)	Lake	Seal
Border(s)	Manufacturing (-ture)	Climate	Homestead Act	Red River Valley
Dakota Territory	Northern Pike		Sioux (Siouan)	Theodore Roosevelt
Pembina	Fort Mandan	Tribes	Louisiana Territory	Pow-wow(s)
Missouri Plateau	Railroad(s)	Cattle	Crops	Prairie(s)

North Dakota Bingo: Card No. 21

North Dakota Bingo

Fur Trade	Livestock	Manufacturing (-ture)	Bismarck	Fargo
River(s)	Mined	Western Wheatgrass	Homestead Act	Badlands
County (-ies)	Judicial Branch		Red River Valley	Ladybug(s)
Tribes	Louisiana Territory	Prairie(s)	Agriculture (-al)	Nokota Horse(s)
Railroad(s)	Crops	Sioux (Siouan)	Dakota Territory	Missouri Plateau

North Dakota Bingo: Card No. 22

North Dakota Bingo

Climate	Sioux (Siouan)	Fort Mandan	Bismarck	Cattle
Bison	Great Plains	Northern Pike	Motto	Agriculture (-al)
Livestock	Fargo		Teredo Petrified Wood	Red River Valley
Dakota Territory	Railroad(s)	Tribes	Crops	Prairie(s)
Seal	White Butte	Pow-wow(s)	Pembina	Manufacturing (-ture)

North Dakota Bingo

Climate	Pow-wow(s)	Great Plains	Sioux (Siouan)	Homestead Act
Manufacturing (-ture)	Cattle	Nokota Horse(s)	River(s)	Red River Valley
Ladybug(s)	Fur Trade		Fargo	Dakota Territory
Seal	Teredo Petrified Wood	Tribes	Crops	Border(s)
Union	Missouri Plateau	Railroad(s)	Mined	White Butte

North Dakota Bingo

Missouri Plateau	Nokota Horse(s)	Sioux (Siouan)	Theodore Roosevelt	Louisiana Territory
Agriculture (-al)	Border(s)	Motto	Climate	Badlands
Livestock	Homestead Act		Teredo Petrified Wood	Tribes
Western Wheatgrass	Seal	White Butte	Railroad(s)	Judicial Branch
Cattle	Great Plains	County (-ies)	Executive Branch	Union

North Dakota Bingo

Manufacturing (-ture)	Sioux (Siouan)	Livestock	River(s)	Fur Trade
Pembina	Mined	Homestead Act	Great Plains	Climate
Louisiana Territory	Teredo Petrified Wood		Judicial Branch	Missouri Plateau
Crops	Bismarck	Seal	Railroad(s)	Tribes
Ladybug(s)	Executive Branch	Theodore Roosevelt	White Butte	Union

North Dakota Bingo: Card No. 26

North Dakota Bingo

Livestock	County (-ies)	Sioux (Siouan)	Great Plains	Legislative Assembly
Seal	Teredo Petrified Wood	Motto	Tribes	Badlands
Grand Forks	White Butte		Railroad(s)	Missouri Plateau
Fur Trade	Bison	Nokota Horse(s)	Union	Agriculture (-al)
Executive Branch	Judicial Branch	Manufacturing (-ture)	Western Wheatgrass	Ladybug(s)

North Dakota Bingo: Card No. 27

North Dakota Bingo

Livestock	Great Plains	Western Wheatgrass	Sioux (Siouan)	Climate
Legislative Assembly	Manufacturing (-ture)	Teredo Petrified Wood	River(s)	Judicial Branch
White Butte	Dakota Territory		Ladybug(s)	Pembina
Western Meadowlark	Fur Trade	Northern Pike	Railroad(s)	Tribes
Bismarck	Lewis and Clark	Executive Branch	Union	Seal

North Dakota Bingo: Card No. 28

North Dakota Bingo

Manufacturing (-ture)	Great Plains	Fur Trade	Motto	Lewis and Clark
Prairie(s)	Pembina	Nokota Horse(s)	Ladybug(s)	Western Wheatgrass
Louisiana Territory	Teredo Petrified Wood		Badlands	Sioux (Siouan)
Legislative Assembly	Seal	Milk	Railroad(s)	Tribes
Climate	Homestead Act	Union	Bison	White Butte

North Dakota Bingo: Card No. 29

North Dakota Bingo

Drift Prairie	Sioux (Siouan)	River(s)	Lewis and Clark	Tribes
Agriculture (-al)	Great Plains	Livestock	Judicial Branch	Badlands
Louisiana Territory	Fargo		Ladybug(s)	Nokota Horse(s)
Union	Bison	Bismarck	Railroad(s)	Teredo Petrified Wood
Seal	Wild Prairie Rose	White Butte	Manufacturing (-ture)	Western Wheatgrass